AF614476

Praise for *Rules of Hunger*

"In reading Lois Roma-Deeley's first book of poems, *Rules of Hunger*, I am struck by the careful precision of her observations....Roma-Deeley marshals these observations in the service of a threshold experience: that moment when you put your hand on the door and then, taking the risk, you push through into the unknown. The poems in *Rules of Hunger* take us through, and we go willingly."

—Peter Huggins, *Phi Kappa Phi Forum*

"In this debut poetry collection, the voice cascades from knowing to wonder and back again. The poet uses poetry as a tool to celebrate both triumphs and defeats. It is a mirror as well as a shroud."

—*ForeWord Magazine*

"One poem in this collection opens with the line, 'Sliding over these days, peeling shadows off my heart'; a second poem closes with the question, 'I ask, again, what takes us/to and from our dreams.' These remarkable lines set the stage for this shadow-play book of poems, whose offerings gift the reader with glimpses of a literal peeling away of the narrator's layers of experience. These poems create a mosaic of hard joy."

—Alberto Ríos, Author of eight books of poetry; National Book Award Finalist; Winner of the Western Literature Association's Distinguished Achievement Award, the Edward Stanley Award for poetry, and the Walt Whitman Award

"*Rules of Hunger* is a book in praise of noble gestures and honorable lives. It is also a book of deep longing and obsession. With a sure and savvy voice, Roma-Deeley travels these two roads at once: the daily path of the ordinary life and the visceral highway that delivers us from the familiar. In between we meet the ancestors, the dreamers, the lovers, and the burning door of sorrow. *Rules of Hunger* is rich with the contradiction and wild dimension that makes us human."

—Jan Beatty, Author of *Mad River* and *Boneshaker* (University of Pittsburgh Press); Winner of the Agnes Lynch Starrett Poetry Prize and the Pablo Neruda Prize for Poetry; host and producer of Prosody, a public radio show on NPR affiliate WYEP-FM featuring the work of national writers

"In 1990 Bill Baer founded *The Formalist, A Journal of Metrical Poetry.* When he had seen it, the playwright Arthur Miller wrote him, *I am sure I will not be the only one who will be grateful for it. Frankly, it was a shock to realize, as I looked through the first issue, that I had very nearly given up the idea of taking pleasure from poetry.* That is the trouble with American poets these days — they have forgotten how to entertain the reader. The result is that no one reads poetry these days because it isn't fun anymore. That's why running across someone like Lois Roma-Deeley is soul-satisfying. Her new book of poetry titled *Rules of Hunger* is not only readable, it is enjoyable to read. She is a paisan' — but not only that. She is a paisan' who can conjure up a world in words. You don't believe me? Look at this from 'The Apostle of Wax and Shine':

> 'If St. Paul should ever lose his way
> on this road that leads through 1959,
> to my seven-year-old self sitting on the front steps
> staring into the nothingness that would become my future,
> he would find a rag top convertible and my father
> the Apostle of Wax and Shine.'

Just perfect."

—Lewis Turco, founding director of both the Cleveland State University Poetry Center and the Program in Writing Arts at S.U.N.Y. Oswego, author of more than 40 books of various kinds including, *The Book of Forms: A Handbook of Poetics* (Dutton, 1968 & University Press of New England, 2000); winner of the Poetry Society of America's Melville Cane Award for literary criticism for *Visions and Revisions of American Poetry* (University of Arkansas Press, 1986); winner, with his Italian translator Joseph Alessia, of the first annual Bordighera Bilingual Poetry Prize for his *A Book of Fears* (Bordighera, 1998); winner of the John Ciardi Award for lifetime achievement in poetry sponsored by the National Italian American Foundation (1999).

"These poems deliciously tilt our equilibrium inside the private lives we long for. Lois Roma-Deeley's bright visual effects infuse her narratives with tender and tough compassion. One of Anne Sexton's gifts to us revealed that the dramatis personae of domestic life feed us in a disappearing act of human transmogrification. Roma-Deeley is alert to danger, yes, but she also assures us that hunger not only commands us, but guides and feeds us. Phoenix and Sicily could not otherwise coincide so well! 'The spinning world/laughs' and in this book of beset perceptions and retrievals, we are beloved guests at the celebration."

—Judith Vollmer, Author of *Reactor* (University of Wisconsin Press, Spring 2004); *The Door Open to the Fire*, winner of the Cleveland State Poetry Prize; *Level Green*, winner of the Brittingham Prize in Poetry; Co-editor of *5 AM*

"The poems in Lois Roma-Deeley's first collection, *Rules of Hunger*, often start in the rich world of the family (Italian, in Roma-Deeley's case) with its legacy of sorrow as well as humor. Then in scintillate, sudden leaps, they take us *elsewhere*. 'North of Babylon,' for example, moves from a childhood city 'built with more walls than/gates' to the haunting image of a woman seeing 'an argument of opening doors.' I'm utterly compelled by how wondrously, again and again, Roma-Deeley goes from the generally observable to the specifically abstract. This is a startling and beautiful debut collection."

—Cynthia Hogue, Author of *Flux*; the Jonathan and Maxine Marshall Chair in Modern and Contemporary Poetry, Arizona State University

"Lois Roma-Deeley's powerful poems are born from danger into a dangerous world, where 'plastic doves pile around your knees' in the Kay-Bee store, each bird 'lying on its broken back.' These finely crafted poems immerse us in the effects of growing up 'on the other side of town.' "

—Jill Breckenridge, Author of *Civil Blood* and *How To Be Lucky*; Winner of the Bluestem Award; National Book Critics' Circle Award nominee

"Through the twin lenses of grief and joy, *Rules of Hunger* examines one woman's childhood and her subsequent removal to a contemporary desertified Arizona; from the combined images of that particular gaze, Lois Roma-Deeley creates meaning. These are poems rich in content, muscular in their form and strange in the way all good art is strange. The poems of Lois Roma-Deeley are fierce, pared down and essential and accomplish the greatest of poetic tasks, which is to document—with care and precision—the lives and deaths of those whom we love."

—Mark Wunderlich, Author of *The Anchorage*, winner of the Lambda Literary Award

Rules of Hunger

~poems~

Rules of Hunger

~poems~

Lois Roma-Deeley

Star Cloud Press
Scottsdale, Arizona

Rules of Hunger

cover art by Beth Shadur
book and cover design by Retha Elmhorst

Published by

~Star Cloud Press~

an imprint of
Cloudbank Creations, Inc.

6137 East Mescal Street
Scottsdale, Arizona 85254-5418

ISBN: 0-9651835-5-6

Library of Congress Control Number: 2004101955

Printed by Lightning Source
La Vergne, TN

For Peter, always

Table of Contents

Part I

Part II

Part III

Part I

My heart
is an open

mouth.

— Jill Breckenridge

Rules of Hunger

Lois Roma-Deeley

2

North of Babylon

Wanting to understand   not/ so/ very/ much
why this city was built with more walls than
gates   but needing someone to explain just how
you walk through the dust   how you look down
at both feet   without wonder   how you stand
under a crumbling archway and   look up
like   you   really   mean it   Tell me what hand
pressed to the middle of my back allowed
me to pass through   Was it yours? A shove   a shout
and suddenly I'm outside   A woman
in sequined heels   A woman old enough
to be somebody's lover   And then/ the land
filled with smoke and fire   And then I ran
from the burning woods   into another town/
there was just one street and some barking hounds
I saw/an argument/ of opening doors   And
leaning against a wall   I touch the gun   the one
I stole from someone's back pocket

Rules of Hunger

Lois Roma-Deeley

The Given

Everyone is out of work. In Phoenix
it's been summer for a very long time.
We're living in a green brick house, rented
to us by a mid-western couple who
never met "EYE-talions" but who know we're clean
enough. My father will die in two years.
My brother will stop drinking. And my husband
will find a good job. I'll go to school and
get a degree. Mom won't stop breathing
for a long while. But right now there is not
much to eat. And our kids want something sweet.
My father looks deep into their faces,
smiles like the gambler I've known him
to be, and says: *Would you like a few plums?*
And then my father turns and looks at me.

Plums should be cold,
in a glass bowl and offered to children.
This is his simple goodness,
the sword to keep on your back, the one
to scrape away the pain of not knowing
what we're to do next or how we're going to act.
And it's just like him to say this in a poem
I never intended to write. Like an *amen*
after a prayer, he invites you to stop
at the doorway of our past
and step into our home.

Rules of Hunger

Lois Roma-Deeley

Inside the Rush of Plastic Pink Wings

Whatever there is that refuses love runs
wild in the aisles of a Kay-Bee store;

Even before the blue-cuffed hand clamped down on your neck,
you started to sweat. Under a shower of plastic doves

falling out of their boxes, dropping
from the supply shelf above the back door

you still weren't sure. What thief calls security,
pulls the alarm? Your stomach heaves. You start to leave

but something pulls you back into the store. The doves
pile up around your knees. Cellophane taunts you.

Tell me, was it more
the thin black line of their full smiles?

or their glittering beaks? Their rosebud eyes
seem to bloom inside the reaches of your head

like simple statements of fact. Was it that
hush of plastic pink wings after my fingers

flicked each one of them off your chest; the twittering
stillness of a bird lying on its broken back?

Rules of Hunger

Lois Roma-Deeley

8

Living In a House Without Furniture

At the very bottom of a dead-end street,
our two-story all-brick three-bedroom house.
My mother, father, grandmother, two brothers

and me. A few memories of Sicily, Roma. No pictures
on the wall. A black and white TV in the basement.
There is a small peach tree, grown from a pit
in fine dirt and coffee grinds saved in a can.
A grandfather's idea of the future.
There are liquor bottles filled with light brown syrup.
This will fool the priest when he comes.
It looks just like good Scotch, my mother says
and no one disagrees. Today
it is Sunday. The house breathes in

tomato sauce simmering on the stove.
Provolone cheese. My Aunt Kitty
comes all the way from Brooklyn
stuffing eggplants and asking me this:
What do you want to be when you grow up?
I'm walking across the living room
with two books on my head. She tells me:
Sii orgogliosa e tira diritto!
 Non guardare mai indietro.
The living room echoes. I want to get down on one knee
and growl out my despair like Louie Prima:
and down and down I go/all around I go/
like a leaf that's caught in a tide...

but all I do is drag my socks, folding the toes under
until I can slide across the bare wood floors,
effortlessly. *Don't you want to be a movie star?*
Have all those people look at you? Say you're pretty?

I say no. I say I don't know.
My eyes don't see well in fading afternoon light,
but it's the shadows that tell me she's crying
and nothing will ever make it all right.

Lois Roma-Deeley

Compulsions (& Obsessions)

There is a hall with seven doors you need to shut; a crystal bowl that makes you think of winter light. In your hand these charms fall open at the slightest touch; a figure fills the middle of the room. Against the white wall, kneel and stack some paper cups. Like a pyramid or a Chinese kite, the blood rises as you count the ways of how and much this child of fortune doesn't want to choose. And new lemons in their yellow skins you have to cut into a dozen eyes that will outshine the night. See how the silver knives and smiling spoons line up. But before the crossword puzzle fills in right, you'll calculate worlds of twirling dust and polish all those pairs of high heel shoes.

Rules of Hunger

Lois Roma-Deeley

Refuge

Let us pretend it exists, this
imaginary forest. And
a woman in a peasant dress
who pulls the hem into a flower around her
head. The full
sound of tambourines and dancing girls
who sing with ribbons of cool pine
shadows. In this picture
the woman remains kind.
The sky is now a circle
of blue. She turns.
The spinning world
laughs.

Rules of Hunger

Lois Roma-Deeley

Because You

Call all bad drivers "Jack" and everybody else "Mac" and because
that never made any sense to me.

Because you bailed my younger brother out of jail, getting up
in the middle of the night and because of you there is honey in the
closet, stamps in the drawer.

Because, when you are angry, you have eyes like cut lemons,
and make the sound that oboes make when they are set on fire,
because you leave your shoes in the middle of the floor.

Rules of Hunger

Lois Roma-Deeley

Storytelling

I’m in the airport watching the clouds
roll onto a tarmac sky. Resistance
was the lesson you said I had missed.
And now, in missing you, I somehow
fail this final test in which I’m pulled down,
in which you knot my hand into a bony fist
and scrape it against blue heaven. You insist
this has to be done. I am screaming out loud
but no one hears me. You’d expect no less
from someone with so little self-respect–
even though you know I can’t ever tell
who kicked the knife across our kitchen floor,
who stood up and walked out the back door.

Rules of Hunger

Lois Roma-Deeley

Piece Work

(i)

Before I was born
my grandmother bought a chalk statue: the *Sacred Heart of Jesus.*
This figure, showing now every crack and nick of my life,
reveals a Jesus, head to waist, pulling open his chest.
There are three holes in each hand, each shaped like a brown rose.
There are two holes for taper candles. Prayers
and wax stains from long ago.
His blue eyes stare into mine. I wonder what he is thinking.
Do the wounds still hurt? Does it hurt to pull at his own flesh?
At the base, an inscription reads: *I will bless*
every place where an image of my heart shall be exposed and venerated.

In the bedroom we shared when I was a girl,
she hung a small picture of the Virgin Mary holding the baby Jesus.
Both Mary and Jesus are sitting on white clouds,
floating above a sea of flames.
In the flames, tortured souls twist and reach out.
Smiling Mary holding a chubby, but thoughtful, baby Jesus.
So serene. So holy. So perfect.
Because of this picture, and
because Mama is old, I want to know
what heaven is really like.
I want to know how death feels.
Is it like walking through a door or falling down the stairs?
These questions—about dying and passing over
and God and Mary and the baby Jesus and all those very unhappy,
very tortured souls swimming in that lake of fire—
make my grandmother very angry.
Why do you want to know? Do you want me to die?

Rules of Hunger

Lois Roma-Deeley

24 Suffolk Avenue

No one has seen you it is past midnight.
The police car drives around the block Once twice
you've /looked/ over /your shoulder
Eyes on the sidewalk circles like blue chalk
In this suburb children play hide and seek
they still play games of it
while you/ have been /wandering for hours
searching for the perfect gift
After the last train dropped you
at the final stop you knew better
but got off and just started walking
Home was never like this Yet you see a house
white with two stories. In the window
a girl stares down and you wave But the drapes close
like/ a/ face/ you /thought/ you knew
Unmoving/ in the false moonlight
you don't want to know
why they are asking you to remove both shoes/
lie face down in the dirt//
why someone is saying *now you understand*
how it works.

Rules of Hunger

Lois Roma-Deeley

The Dot Above the i

For Allen Woodman

Seeing and not being seen, moving
among and in between, playing
like a musical note let loose
in the wild summer air. This

is not the magic of which we spoke.
This is more like a pair of green chairs
emptying in the sun, the paint peeling
under the thumb–you never answered
my question: *How much?*
or was it *why is there such*
inconsistency? Will you please tell me
what did you see when I asked you:

Look into the lights lining the streets
of Kansas City.

Rules of Hunger

Lois Roma-Deeley

Crossing the Desert

At three in the afternoon, the sky in July
over Gila Bend is a holocaust of light.
Yet beyond this heat rising off the asphalt
like a genie in a bottle, the first cliché
of a TV movie where everyone gets killed
before anyone completes a full sentence, there is
a candlewood tree turning.
A train rolls by,
flatbed cars moving toward Phoenix.

Rules of Hunger

Lois Roma-Deeley

The Apostle of Wax and Shine

Parked in our driveway, the big finned
Lincoln sits like a fish
settling at the bottom of a basket
of so many passed-around loaves. As if its wide eyes,
open in death and crusted with chrome, went blind.

If St. Paul should ever lose his way
on this road that leads through 1959,
to my seven-year-old self sitting on the front steps
staring into the nothingness that would become my future,
he would find a rag top convertible, and my father
the Apostle of *Wax and Shine.*

Maybe he would come to understand a man
who's two months behind his $64-a-month house payment;
the black haired, squarish man, with strong teeth and sun-tanned arms
who supports his wife, kids, no-good brother;
who makes the rounds, delivering bananas
in a small truck to little grocery stores
owned by immigrant Jews and Italians;
the sporting man whose name–*Lou*–is inscribed in script on blue denim,
maybe Paul would cut the guy a break.
He might see a man whistling as he rubs the soft cloth
into paste wax and then, onto the white paint,
making circles inside of circles each and every time.
But does he see my own face in the reflection
gleaming the hood of this car? See the wisdom

of four white walls which will spin
into spring, clearing a space across the days,
a very small place where I still live
simply for a little bit of magic?

Rules of Hunger

Lois Roma-Deeley

Part II

The voice is a second face.

— Gerard Bauer

Rules of Hunger

Lois Roma-Deeley

Severe Traffic

I'm already above the speed limit
when this guy behind me hits his horn.

A yellow two-tone pick-up
lets me sideways into line.

We become one snake sliding
over dirt bumps and through a valley

of orange cones. I'm twisting on my seat,
reaching for a map

that's fallen on the floor. Up ahead,
there's a blinking neon sign: *Severe Traffic.*

What were you thinking that night, staring
into the headlights of the yellow cab

that came to take me home?
You're still winding down,

sinking deep into our old sofa in that house
I passed hours ago. Outside your window,

there is a rattling hum to keep me from going on like this,
heart-stopping in the middle of the road.

Rules of Hunger

Lois Roma-Deeley

With Hands on Both Hips

I was smart but not a hood.
Even in hot pink stirrup pants,
without teased beehive and cat's eyes
drawn with black liner to a fine bird wing "V,"
what could I do but hide in my good girl looks,
pursue deception as if it were high art?

Every day I'd swear out loud, practice:
Bitch! Bitchen! Goddamsonofabitch!
Every night I'd read my poetry books,
talk secret talk to Emily and Walt.

Before the mirror starts to clear
there's the likeness of a girl
much too smart for her own good.

Rules of Hunger

Lois Roma-Deeley

Piece Work

(ii)

Even now, she is watching me, watching me.

Mama couldn't read or write, Italian or English.
Her drunk of a father beat her
as she was sneaking off to night school.
Puttana.
I tell you my grandmother lived until she was 82 without the
comfort of books.

She stands at the picture window all day
looking into the street.
I know she isn't thinking about me. During her life

she learned enough to buy a few good diamonds, to make
four hand crocheted bedspreads and give them
to four daughters, saying:
Someday when I'm gone, you'll remember.

Rules of Hunger

Lois Roma-Deeley

Gestures

i.

There's the old woman standing at check-in
whose hunched shoulders look like a valentine.
A dark man in a dark suit who finds
dinner mints in his jacket, offers one
to the young nun beside him. A couple
of red roses, wrapped in tissue paper,
fall to the floor.

ii.

A tall man sits beside me. His leather case
leans against my thigh. I'm suddenly afraid
of dinner and a movie;
small bars of hotel soap; English tea
with you and the crossword puzzle in *The Times...*
it's not about the double set of blue lines
I want to draw around my entire life,
making a neat box to hold what is right
in front of us–safe. The past is more like
this poor excuse for a train, rattling on
between two fixed points–a bead on a charm–

like some bastard with his eyes staring into mine.

Rules of Hunger

Lois Roma-Deeley

Keeping Quiet In a Jar

There is wind inside
the glass which encircles
an exact replication
of bonsai leaves. Yet when you leave
the room, the tree will seem
to bow. Once outside
you brace against the cold.
Red spots on both cheeks, blood
ringing in your ears, the tops
sting before turning numb. You are alone
wondering if you missed something
inside that shop, the glass jar,
the smiling man.

Rules of Hunger

Lois Roma-Deeley

Too Many Ghosts

This is the best
you can do? I say, *You call*
this a haunting?
I'm standing near the stove–*stirring*
things up–they chatter away
while I cook, make my head
ache. These are only onions,
for God's sake. Not layers
of memories. Not even
Uncle Link's hand on the knife,
chopping sausage for the stuffing,
will make me stop turning
from the still pictures that rise
up from the bottom of my
grandmother's pot. She is not
happy. Again I've forgotten
to salt the water. *And now,*
says Aunt Mae, *the baked Ziti*
will be floppy. My father
frowns. His only daughter
should know better. My cousin
Freddy starts another story.
Sometimes, in the steam
of artichokes, I see a round
dining room table with cane back
chairs, and these people are shouting:
We're not very dead. Uncle
Ray, drinking his everlasting
Scotch, just laughs. *Now this*
is really heaven.

Rules of Hunger

Lois Roma-Deeley

Looking For a Street Sign

I've been counting backward since we left St. Louis.
Nine Cities. Four Bridges. Two Streets
divided into smaller streets, unbroken lines
of yellow paint. Houses on dark corners. Endless
rows of parked cars. My foot tapping the brakes. The scrape
of windshield wipers. Underneath a red awning,
an old man crosses himself. And then, there's a man
in the coffee shop, sipping latte from a mug,
folding the paper back, never once looking up
from his plate. Now I'm wondering how long it takes
one person to stop loving another.
Someone should say I got bad directions.
Someone should shout, pound the table, call for service.
A tired waitress takes down my order:
Hey honey, she says, what won't you have?

Rules of Hunger

Lois Roma-Deeley

Two Women Appear to Listen to the Talk of Men

Don't you just want to die? Every time he goes on like this, like
I'm some swollen river he has to get across before
the tides sweep him away and there he is,
clinging to the barest branch with, no doubt,
water filling his mouth, his lungs and,
if he takes just one more breath, he'll drown in the darkest part of my eye.

You know, there isn't any reason why you just couldn't cry out right now
        "Get Away From Me"–
There would be a pause. Then the other one might step back, dig his heels
        against the wall and
look up. On the ceiling, there might be widow ghosts and giant spiders....

Of course, if we speak now they will only feel the unease of women
who know how to bring the evening to an abrupt end;
to the silence of mothers standing at a split rail fence,
aprons slung low on wide hips, hair pulled back into a tight "o," the words
written in lipstick on their foreheads: this will never get said.

Rules of Hunger

Lois Roma-Deeley

Passport

Just for today, I'm speaking
Italian to stray dogs and sullen cats.
Ciao, Bella! Come stai?
When the sky is this water lily blue
I think of my mother. Today I decided
dying must be something like that–
a series of sounds, sharp or flat,
unattached to meaning. But the feeling
of *I-ought-to-know* whose teeth marks
stripped the tree bark white with fury
brings me back to how
an ordinary life will leave us.

Rules of Hunger

Lois Roma-Deeley

"Money Doesn't Care Who Has It"

Seven dollars on the kitchen counter.
Here's a little something for you...
he whispered into her just-washed hair
...to help with your education.
He laughed and left. Later, I counted
every bill while sitting on the bed.
Barbie and Ken were looking out the window.
This much I have learned:
the world can turn on a thin dime,
swallow everything you know.

Rules of Hunger

Lois Roma-Deeley

The White Line

She sits and snaps her peas: *just once*
he could have smiled....when the end
of his trowel kept tap, tap, tapping and she–
thinking it was one of her new found friends–
yelled: *Come on in!* Her husband's lips, fine and thin,
press into a long white line.

Beside the acacia, on a stone bench,
she sits in her garden. Just the snail vines
talk to her now. Those low, sweet voices
that came to visit must have been from God:
They spread their fingers before flying
over house and willow tree; they stroke
their billowing sleeves and speak to her;
they pass through time.

The sun in her lap feels like a hole through which
she is falling. Like a deer in the wilderness
that licks salt and smells the water,
he works to finish and he works to wait.
But it's her garden;
only the wall was his to make.

Rules of Hunger

Lois Roma-Deeley

Two Decks of Cards

Friday night, the weekly pinochle game
my mother's come to hate. Scotch and water

spills into short glasses. Salted peanuts fill a jar.
Strangers at our table. A multitude

of fives, tens, twenties.
Tomorrow she will leave him–

my first train ride, visiting Aunt Fay.
We go to the sea. The sun is shining on the dock.

You don't even know these people. She'll tell him
later when he comes, half-running down the walk.

My mother and I are crabbing. I don't want to leave.
The water is clear. I'm about to put my feet

over the side. My mother's hair is rolled in a red bandanna,
the vein between her eyebrows pulses blue.

Touching her arm, my father whispers, *say it.*

Rules of Hunger

Lois Roma-Deeley

Still Life

The small wings
beat stillness out of the air.
Like the buzz of a street light, you're startled and look.
There should be something in your hand, some sweet thing.
It rose above the roof and flew into the trees.

A single hummingbird. There is a sound–
here is the fear to carry you through
the dark tunnel of the year. The bird's eye
opens–infinite
as the possibility of turning
down a city block at midnight and finding–
on the basement wooden window sill, green apples
in a bowl which, everyone knows, are meant
just for you. Only for you.

Rules of Hunger

Lois Roma-Deeley

Blind Alley, Black Holes

Can't you feel it?
In the smell of roasting potatoes. In the taste of rubber balls.
In your own palm, the time line bends before it ends.

We have no word for *oblivion*/that is quite/
accurate?

Fear your murmuring heart, fear loaves of bread uneaten, fear
        your own hand
on the window sill before dark, fear that hesitation seen in the
        shadows of children
walking home from school.

Don't be afraid.

Fear of nothingness doesn't exist–
Yet you continue to insist. It's erased from the list of concerns.
We've replaced records.
Rewound the clock.
Invented new seasons.
We have systems....

Aren't you bored yet? Sick of your own voice? I say to you
walk down this blind alley.
With black holes in the bottom of my shoes?

Rules of Hunger

Lois Roma-Deeley

It's a Haunting of Shifting Sun

Sliding over these days, peeling shadows off my heart.
My whole life is a slice of onion held to the light.

Once I took the subway to your house.
Wrought iron
and two pots of half-blooming geraniums
waited. See how it happens?

See how
it's happening again:
The emptying street below the El.
A tunnel to walk through.
Now all I have to do is turn
the corner, jump inside a yellow cab
then, take the steps two at a time,
close my eyes and lean my head
against the cool blue metal door.

Rules of Hunger

Lois Roma-Deeley

Part III

Art is our chief means of breaking bread with the dead.

— W. H. Auden

Rules of Hunger

Lois Roma-Deeley

Pages You Wrote

In 1976, you were
feeling kind of blue. The top loops
of your *H's* and *G's* became
nooses where all those errant thoughts
would be stilled. No one should be caught
by a marriage that is not working.
Then, in '82, you press deep
red into the paper. Your child,
born without a limb, is walking.
While my father was dying, you wrote
in black. By the 1990's
your sentences were but a word
or two.

Rules of Hunger

Lois Roma-Deeley

Rules of Hunger

It will be a feast you refuse to eat
and enjoy. Somehow I will offend you
with a plate of stuffed mushrooms and a side
of imported cheese. Tonight
you're a guest in my house.
I pass the rolls while you tap each wine glass
with your fork. I'll make small talk
over cold shrimp and a lobster bisque.
Why should this hurt me?
Someone calls for an aperitif.
I drop strawberries into a champagne glass.
You stare at the napkin, these thin creases
made by a narrow thumb.
There's an attempt to pass the caviar
but you shake both shoulders
and laugh.

Rules of Hunger

Lois Roma-Deeley

Counting

What gave it away? The graffiti on the wall?
The red headed twin you saw race around the block? Twice
you heard a baby scream; two clay pots a boy pushes off
the second story window scared you; you step through the door
onto familiar concrete. A young couple kiss, then fight.
You close both eyes–you always close your eyes–disliking the light
blue neon circles under the billboards which say this time
you should take note, write it down, notice–*I've been here before.*
Maybe it was all that counting. Streets. Trees. Men in flowered
shirts. Those hands disappearing inside your pocket. You squeeze
through the alley way, running like it meant something. It rains
down your throat. Why won't you remember? First left, *then* right.
Put your feet on the sidewalk. Walk. Turn the corner. You think
nothing can't be taken from nothing–just keep moving.

Rules of Hunger

Lois Roma-Deeley

(Just For Today) I'm Stealing Your Story

for Cookie Ann

Let me outline it for you, the tale of Kool-Aid and Fruit Loops.
It's about summer and Phoenix, the way the desert
smells of creosote and coyotes who, on really bad nights,
eat your cats. This is the short form, the list of characters:
teenage girls shoving you against the locker, beating
you up; a mother who, for nine years, keeps forgetting
to tell you she's divorced your father until
you *just had to ask*; your father
who never quite makes it all the way home but who flies planes
above your house–*Wave to Daddy!*–I've seen the picture.
There's two TVs in the living room.
The console and the portable on top of the console.
Both are broken.
Except for the night you and your sister hear the console
come on by itself, and there is Carol Burnett, and then it's two in
    the morning
and you are both sick from laughing and finally fall asleep knowing
this will never work again. I hope I got that part right.
There are books which tell you how to live.
There's *Rosemont*, a pretend school.
And, of course, there's Danny
the boy you love. One day you go to college, take a class
and there's a woman sitting in the front row;
she refuses to turn around, to speak a word.
And then it's 20 years and then it's just me
and you and this page which can't seem to say we
know this is not the end of the story.

Rules of Hunger

Lois Roma-Deeley

Las Vegas, 1982

Can you feel it? He asks me
as I lean over the craps table
in the Star Dust, throw the dice, backhanded,
against the green felt. My father
believes in luck. *Snake eyes:*

cancer eats both lungs.

Rules of Hunger

Lois Roma-Deeley

Because You #2

Rice paper dancing over a snow lawn.
Neon arrows blinking along the highway.
Cedar pressed into the plaid of cotton flannel lapels.

That breath in the end of a very long sentence.
Hummingbirds at the ledge of an open window.
Ice at the bottom of a very tall glass.

I am not a beacon or a bell–
Not the complaint of morning hours
Not the nothing of what is

Rules of Hunger

Lois Roma-Deeley

Milking Goats Upside Down Somewhere In a Foreign Country

In my last dream, your whole face was floating
on the water. This time your voice is still,
clouds passing over the field stop, then dark spots
appear on the slope of the hill. Circles in air
grow inside each other. Dust rises up.
Across the plain of wheat there is a tin pail.
Ma, you smell of tea roses and lemonade.
The day is warm. It must be summer.
Beside me, Peter turns over in bed, stops
the dream, then it starts again

this must be you drifting toward me.
I notice the trail of ants on the sidewalk
ring the milkweed. The eye of a lost tourist
staring straight at me as he leans on the wall,
his chest puffed out, drawn in.
The herd of goats stopping in front of the car.
In the dream, I'm speaking flawless French.
Here you find me wanting to end the night
in an outdoor café with you
drinking a tall Scotch, wearing a red silk scarf
and the singing waiter who only wants to serve you
more ice; *que será, será.*

Rules of Hunger

Lois Roma-Deeley

Lost Hours

I miss your voice
slowing to a deliberate drawl.
I seem to have lost
a young girl whispering to the stone lions.
One shy afternoon when October light
collected on the roses, and that fall
when I remembered to blush just because
I stood outside your front door.
Did you really think I couldn't let go
of a grown man who can only suppose?

Glass chimes will always fall off a maple tree.
I was wrong about lost hours backed into a corner
of a day; that even the sound of a single book closing,
falling to the floor
won't let me forfeit one minute of wanting
your kind of love.

Rules of Hunger

Lois Roma-Deeley

Piece Work

(iii)

My mother told me Francesca Masucci–my grandmother–had a
difficult life–
all her children said she was a difficult person.
Cold. Demanding. Unaffectionate
but not unloving. My mother said we had to respect her.
Everyone in our family respected her.
To me, she never spoke except in the imperative.
In her broken English, she said:
Take out the garbage! Get down! Don't do that! That's a sin!

My cousin who lived two streets down from our family,
who was more like a sister than a cousin,
who was at our house every day when I was growing up—
when I married young and very poor—
wished me luck, saying
you're going to need it.

Rules of Hunger

Lois Roma-Deeley

If the House Roars In the Middle of the Night

You will want to believe in it   the spare   bare
spot on the wall   No one will come   No one will care
Still it may be a sun spot flare   It may be your past
come to the very last turn in your heart   Try
to resist and you are half-way there
on a path within the realm of an ordinary day/ where reason/
doesn't have to watch its back//

It is an ocean of nothingness where
you will breathe in   slowly   the contagion of your life

Rules of Hunger

Lois Roma-Deeley

The Very Thing

Spider webs in my own blood
come from staring too much
at the sun through closed eyelids.
Seeing is not believing.
And I'm finally relieved

this orange ball of light
inside my head is not
particular. Theory
would have it stay balanced
in the air. Forever
circling.

I don't turn away from this burning
even though I know
it shows up, so often
without a name and address,

then leaves me with a streak
of blazing forgetfulness...
still,

like the spaces
in late night conversations
I fill in what I don't know
with wanting.

Every Scrap of Paper

For each day wasted,
make a mark
on the walls in the house
of broken windows. Take
out the brick walk and
cut down the maples.
Leave nothing to chance.
Even the dirt,
taken through the garden
grate. Do not
touch anything. Do not
look over the side fence
between the narrow streets
to where there might still be
a river with a bridge.
Do not expect to see
a face in the water.

Rules of Hunger

Lois Roma-Deeley

Transparent Moon Over Laguna

All last night I asked you nothing
but questions. Who lives in that house
built on a cliff overlooking
the sea? What is the syntax of
checkered table cloth and yellow
umbrellas?

You laughed and handed me a drink.
From your balcony, the bluest
hibiscus. Where has our past brought us?
The beach fills with morning summer
while I try, hard, not to think
the seagulls on the rooftops
or the fog clinging in a ring
around the mountains mean anything.
I ask, again, what takes us
to and from our dreams.

Rules of Hunger

Lois Roma-Deeley

She Is Smiling At the Camera

Now there is only some food and this one poem...
and, moving through the pines of Arizona,
her face in a cloudy breath of winter air.
This is the title page of the thin book
you touch each night. There must be a thousand ways
these filthy creatures can be made to pay
for their sullen looks. You and Jane took
to chasing them from the cabin porch and–
when she died last spring, taking her last
words with her–their eyes seemed to dare you
to leave them alone. The watering can
of red petunias, which she planted in
full sunlight, is rusting with overgrowth.
In the bedroom, there's a picture which shows
you with a full head of hair. She is smiling.
Both of your shoulders touch the wall.
Jack, I will bring you something
to eat. You have let the telephone ring
for hours. Jack, these are not the squirrels
who ate through the hammock and green lawn chairs.

Rules of Hunger

Lois Roma-Deeley

Sun, Table, Chair

As if
that dog barking at the green pear
is a signal to sit right down
and listen. Something wild hangs in the air.
Your mind goes to it.

Hold still just one more minute.
See, over there
underneath the broadleaf and tired tree,
how a small boy is calling you.
He's grown so little in all these years,
you weep. You say *it's something in the air.*

Rules of Hunger

Lois Roma-Deeley

Stupido

I see him standing just inside our front door.
My father in his eternal rain coat
checking out the new house.
Did you know you're dead?
"Yes," he says, "four months now. Nice home,
good choice–you learned well."
What are you doing here?
"I've come for Melissa."

I'm real awake now, running
down the hall. In our daughter's room,
I stare at her small body. In the blue light
from the hallway, I see her chest, rising
up and down. Her lips, drawn down
like a comma, her eyes darting
under paper thin lids. She is still breathing.
I stumble to our bed,

fall back asleep.
"Stupido," my father continues,
and there he is again with rain coat
folded over his arm, water
dripping from his nose onto his hat.
His voice, unbelieving as the cracks
in the wall I've been holding onto.
"I've come to help...

go to sleep now. Get some rest."

Rules of Hunger

Lois Roma-Deeley

On the Other Side of Town

There is a bar
where music plays
all night
and people drink bourbon
before they jitterbug.
Men who smoke thin cigars.
Women whose bare shoulders
dip as they dance. Outside
the sun and crescent moon
slide off the sidewalk and
there is no point to which
anyone can turn.

Rules of Hunger

Lois Roma-Deeley

Missing the Bus

There is a street I had to get across.
Turning the corner, I passed the young men
laughing at my plaid skirt. It snows
lightly on the sidewalk. I prayed to die
before I reach the bus stop. The flakes simply
fade away like a smile I've grown used to.
Under the red awning, a grown woman stands all day
in the rain. And, when the bus finally came,
I looked into the face behind the doors
and signaled–*keep on driving.*

Rules of Hunger

Lois Roma-Deeley

Acknowledgments

Grateful acknowledgment is made to the following publications, in which some of these poems—or versions of these poems—first appeared or earned recognition: *"e"– The 2000 Emily Dickinson Award Anthology* ("Gestures," competition finalist—Universities West Press); *The Emily Dickinson Award Anthology: A Commemorative Edition of the Best Poems of 2001* (" [Just For Today] I'm Stealing Your Story," competition semifinalist—Universities West Press); Tucson Poetry Festival ("The Given," formerly titled "An Impulse of Plums," selected by Maxine Kumin as a featured poem for the Festival Competition); *Controlled Burn* ("Too Many Ghosts"); *A Poetic Dialogue: Poetry:Women:Art* bookmark with Beth Shadur ("Refuge").

I would like to thank Norman Dubie, Rita Dove, Alberto Ríos, Jane Hirshfield, and C.D. Wright.

A special *grazie* to Jill Breckenridge, Cynthia Hogue, Judith Vollmer, and Mark Wunderlich.

My deepest gratitude to Jan Beatty for her generous ordering of the poems in this manuscript.

I would like to thank Steven Swerdfeger, publisher, for his vision; Sydney James, editor, for making me fill up all the blank spaces; Marianne Roccaforte, copy editor, guardian angel of every comma; Beth Shadur, visual artist, for her passion; Retha Elmhorst, cover and book designer, for her talent and great laugh; my students, for their friendship and trust; my PVCC colleagues and friends, especially Jack Sexton, Karen Kabrich, John Nelson, Alan Tongret, Gene Rister, Christopher Scinto, Joan Ritsch, Judi Anderson, Sue Isackson, Rod Fensom and June Hawkins, for their support; Fara Darland and Judy Christensen, for knowing; Nancy Matte, for believing for more than twenty years; Virginia Chase Sutton, for her devotion to poetry; Liz Tregor-Dokken, sister-friend through it all; Marie Pomponio and Ann Wrubel, for standing with me; Carol Faraone and Debra Roma, for never giving up; Patrick Deeley, Jr, for his generosity to the children; Michael Deeley, for loving poetry and having guts; John Deeley, for knowing how to dream; extended family members of the Roma/ Faraone/ Giglio/ Cauldfield/ Heiser/ Winter/ Bruno/ Deeley/ Skorubski/ Carr/ Pomponio/ Wrubel/ Hilliard/ McClelland/ Rothlisberger families, for their love and their history; Nick Faraone, my big brother, for teaching me how to think and for giving me Wordsworth and the French Symbolists; Lou "Bud" Roma, Jr, my little brother, for his kind heart and quick wit; Cecilia Deeley, for that night on the beach when we both knew all things are possible. To Fay Giglio Titone, for her strength. Remembering all my dead relatives who first taught me the art of story telling, especially Ray Giglio, Sr, and Fred Bruno; in memory of Patrick Carr, Patrick Deeley, Sr, and William "Link" Caulfield, good men, and the aunts: Mae Caulfield Watson, Kitty Bruno, and Kitty Skorubski, for their courage. In memory of my grandmother, Frances Masucci, who was beaten for wanting to learn to read and write; and my parents, Lou and Jo Roma, who taught me how to love. To Fr. Eric Tellez, for his wisdom; Cookie Ann and Trixie, for faith and hope; Kyle Rothlisberger, for his brilliant heart; Jody Deeley, for her depth of spirit; Erin Deeley, Kailey Rothlisberger, Allison Deeley, Mariah Rothlisberger and Dylan Rothlisberger, for simply being; Peter Deeley, Jr, and Melissa Deeley Rothlisberger, for everything that can never be put into words; and Peter Deeley, Sr, the love of my life.

Photograph credit: Mary Warner

Lois Roma-Deeley has published in six anthologies, including the American Book Award winner *Looking for Home* (Milkweed Editions), and in numerous literary journals nationwide. Her work has earned awards for outstanding writing, including the 2004 Emily Dickinson Award, and a nomination for the 2003 Arizona Governor's Arts Awards. Poet-in-Residence at Paradise Valley Community College in Phoenix, Arizona, Lois Roma-Deeley holds an M.F.A. (poetry) from Arizona State University and a Ph.D. (poetry) from the Union Institute and University. Roma-Deeley grew up in North Babylon, New York. Currently she lives in Scottsdale, Arizona, with her family. *Rules of Hunger* is her first full-length collection of poetry.

www.ingramcontent.com/pod-product-compliance
Ingram Content Group UK Ltd.
Pitfield, Milton Keynes, MK11 3LW, UK
UKHW041852190726
13854UKWH00002B/851